Bugs in a Log

Written by Michèle Dufresne

PIONEER VALLEY EDUCATIONAL PRESS, INC.

Look at the bug.
The bug is on a **log**.

Look at the bug.
The bug is in the log.

Some logs are hollow. Bugs crawl inside to hide or lay eggs.

The sun **lit** up the log.
Look! The bug naps
in the log.

Light can shine on a log and make it warm. Some bugs love the heat. Many bugs sleep or rest in logs.

The bug **led** lots of bugs
to the log.

Some bugs, like ants, live in groups. One bug may lead the rest to food or back to their home.

I can see a lot of bugs!

There are more bugs on Earth than any other kind of animal. Some logs have hundreds of tiny bugs living inside them!

glossary

log

lit

led